AF269436

Under the Sea

Published in 2024 by Windmill Books,
an Imprint of Rosen Publishing
2544 Clinton St.
Buffalo, NY 14224

Publishing Director Belinda Gallagher
Creative Director Jo Cowan
Editorial Director Rosie Neave
Senior Editor Becky Miles
Design Manager Simon Lee
Production Jenny Brunwin
Image Manager Liberty Newton
Reprographics Stephan Davis
Assets Lorraine King

Cataloging-in-Publication Data

Names: Hardy, Samara, illustrator.
Title: Under the sea / illustrated by Samara Hardy.
Description: New York : Windmill Books, 2024. | Series: Wonderful words
Identifiers: ISBN 9781538394663 (pbk.) | ISBN 9781538394670 (library bound) | ISBN 9781538394687 (ebook)
Subjects: LCSH: Marine animals--Pictorial works--Juvenile literature. |
Marine ecology--Pictorial works--Juvenile literature. |
Vocabulary--Pictorial works--Juvenile literature.
Classification: LCC QL122.2 M554 2024 | DDC 591.77'89--dc23

Printed in the United States of America

CPSIA Compliance Information: Batch CSWM24
For Further Information contact Rosen Publishing at 1-800-237-9932

Find us on 

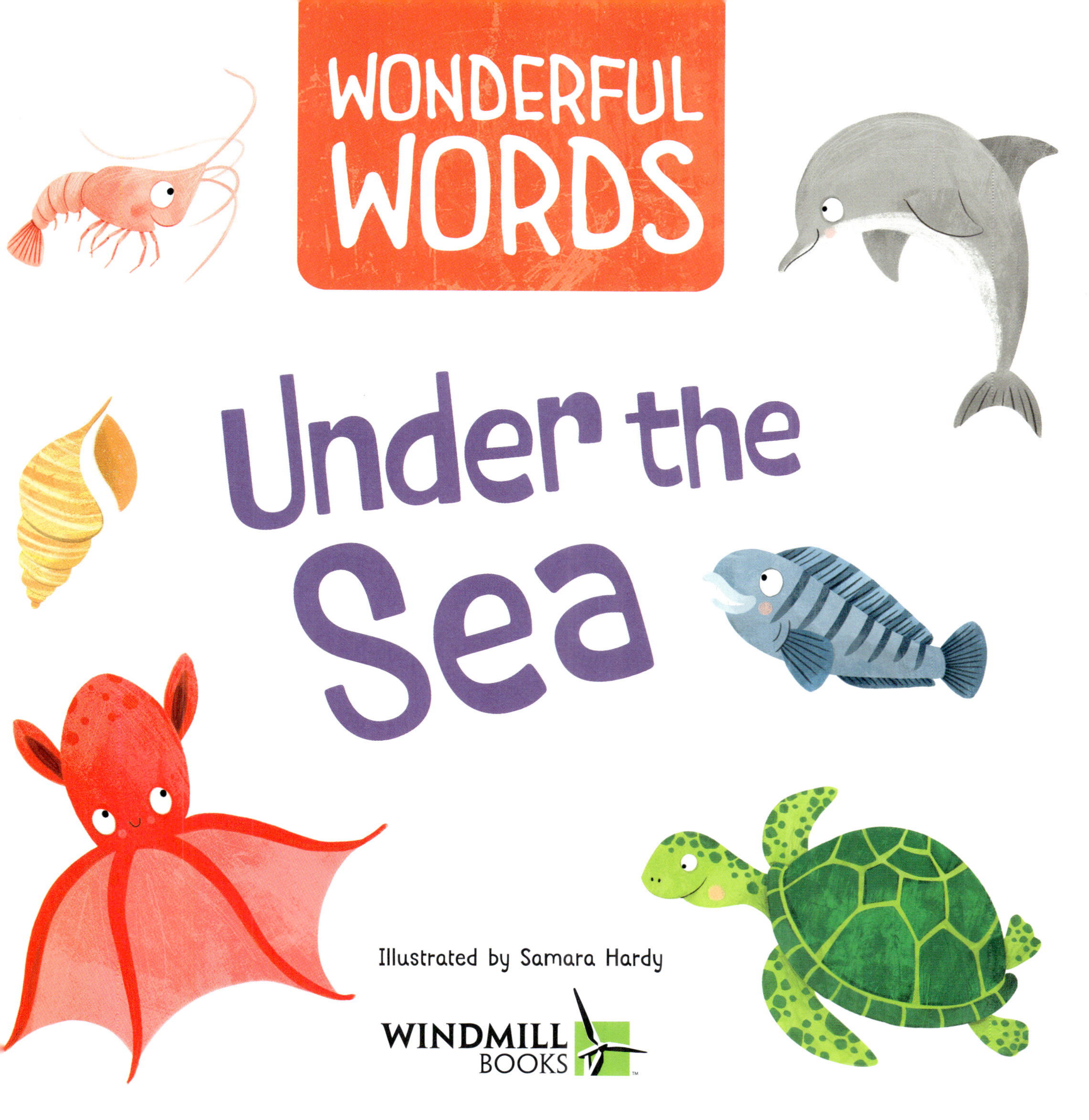

WONDERFUL WORDS
Under the Sea
Illustrated by Samara Hardy
WINDMILL BOOKS

Coral reef

These precious places are home to many different kinds of sea creatures.

stingray
HOW MANY FISH
CAN YOU SEE?
angelfish
pearl
sponge

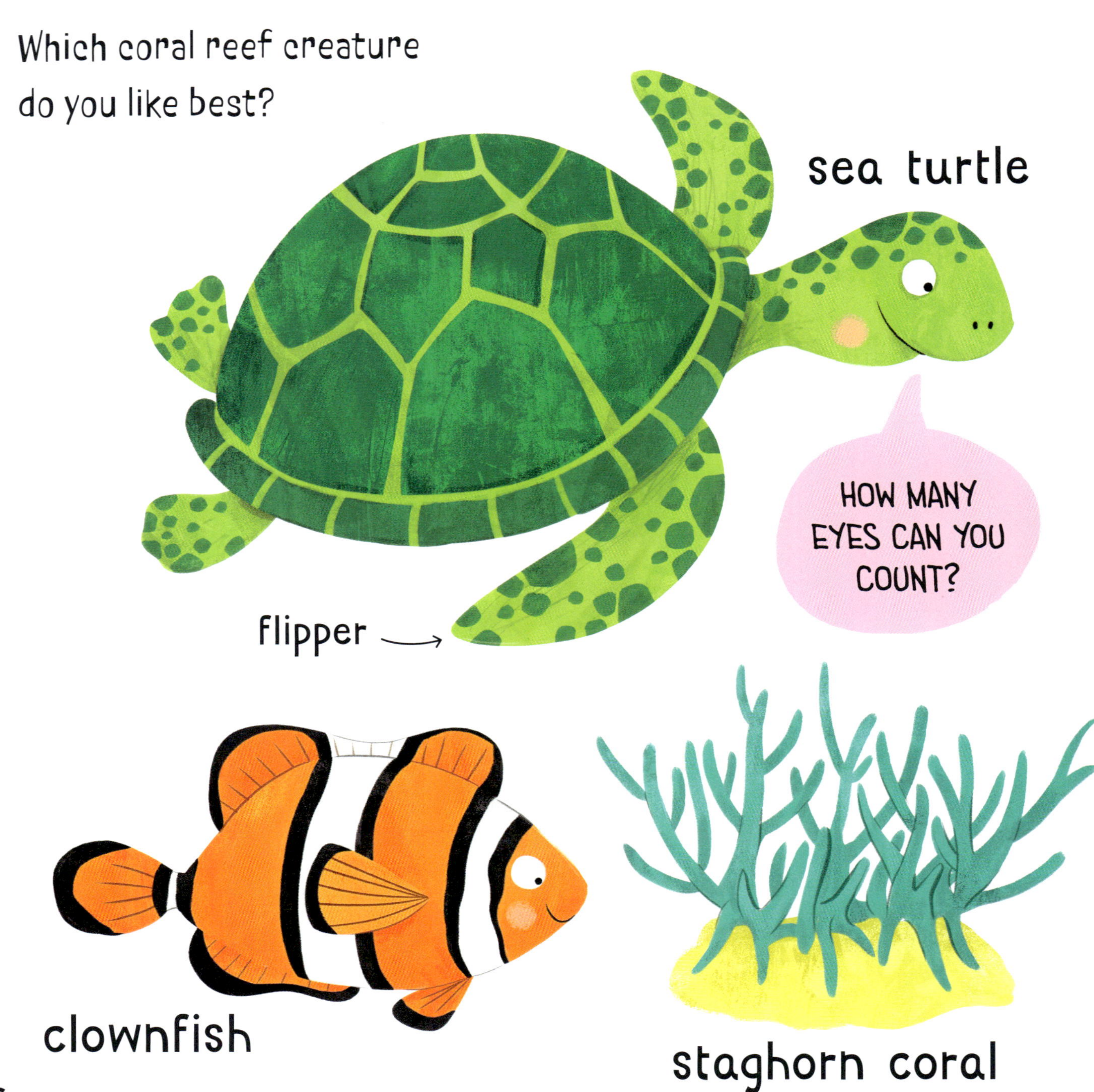

Which coral reef creature
do you like best?
sea turtle
HOW MANY
EYES CAN YOU
COUNT?
flipper
clownfish
staghorn coral

blue tang
fish
seahorse
sea snake
fin
WHICH ANIMALS
CAN YOU SPOT WITH
STRIPES?
reef shark

On the seabed

At the bottom of the sea, fish swim among rocks and seaweed.

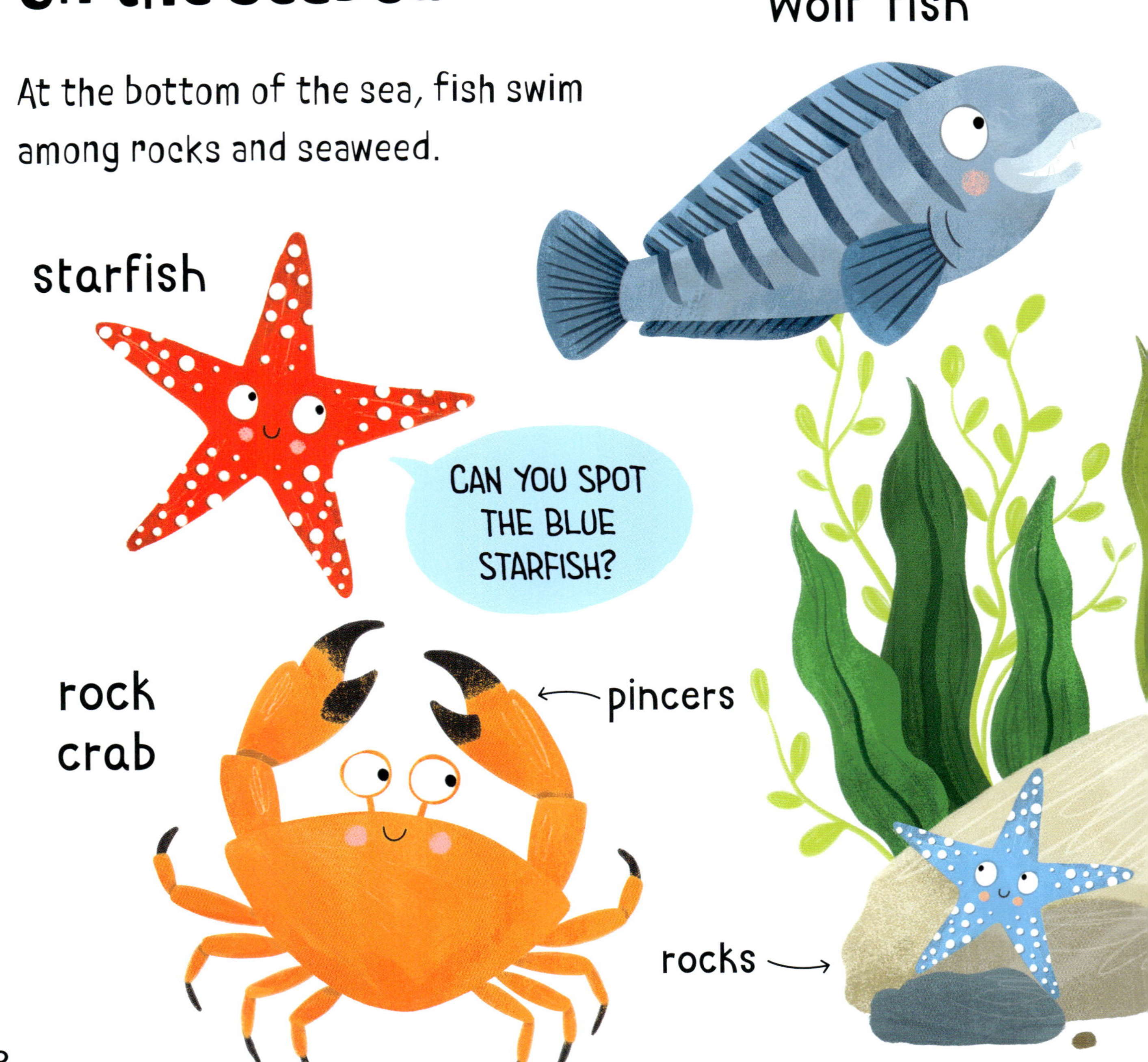

prawn
flounder
shoal
of fish

Lots of unusual-looking animals live
in oceans around the world.
ribbontail
ray
octopus
lobster
claw

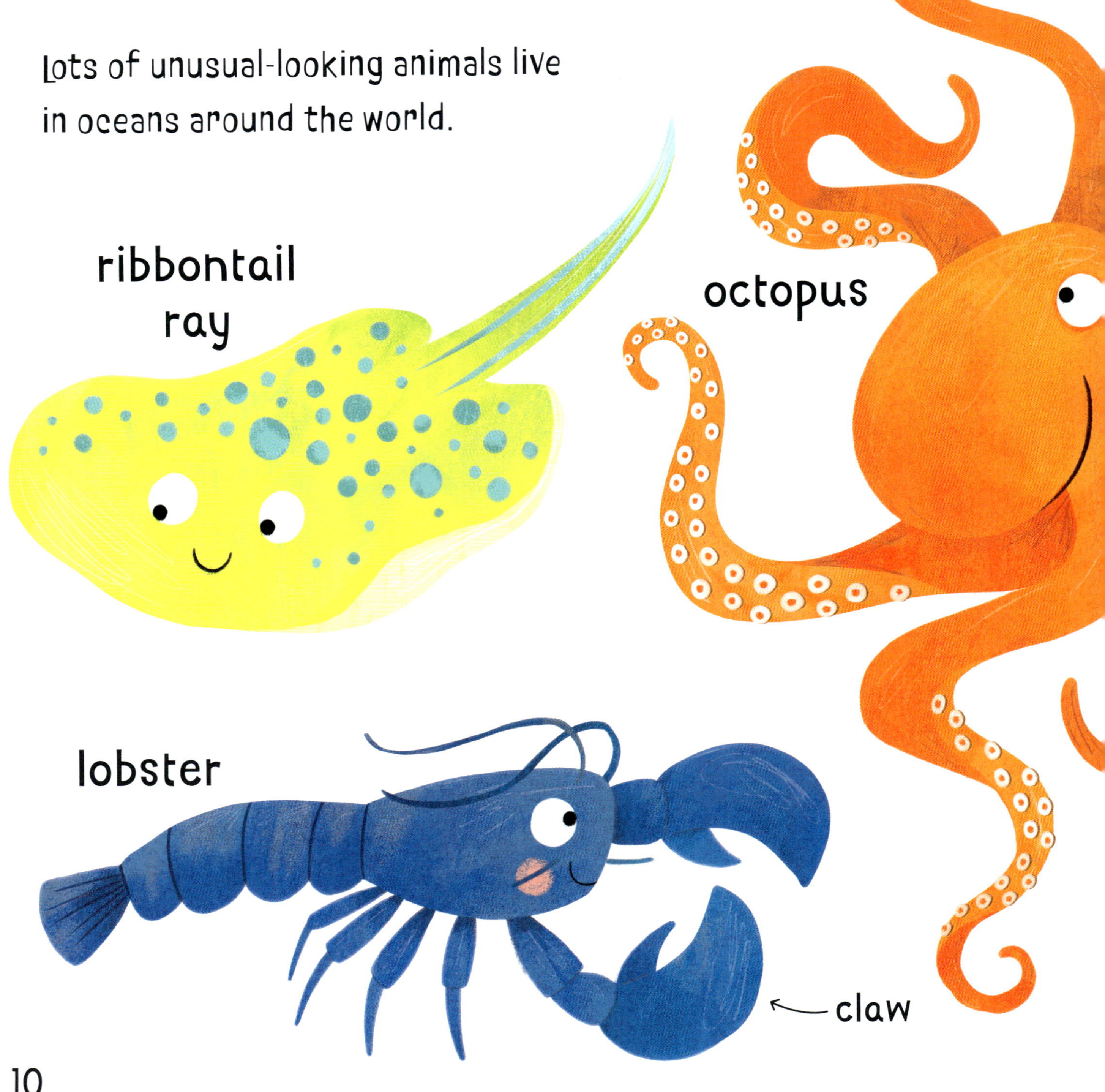

10

suckers
CAN YOU COUNT EIGHT ARMS ON THE OCTOPUS?
jellyfish
tentacles
nurse shark
gills

Wide-open sea

The open ocean is home to big fish and whales.

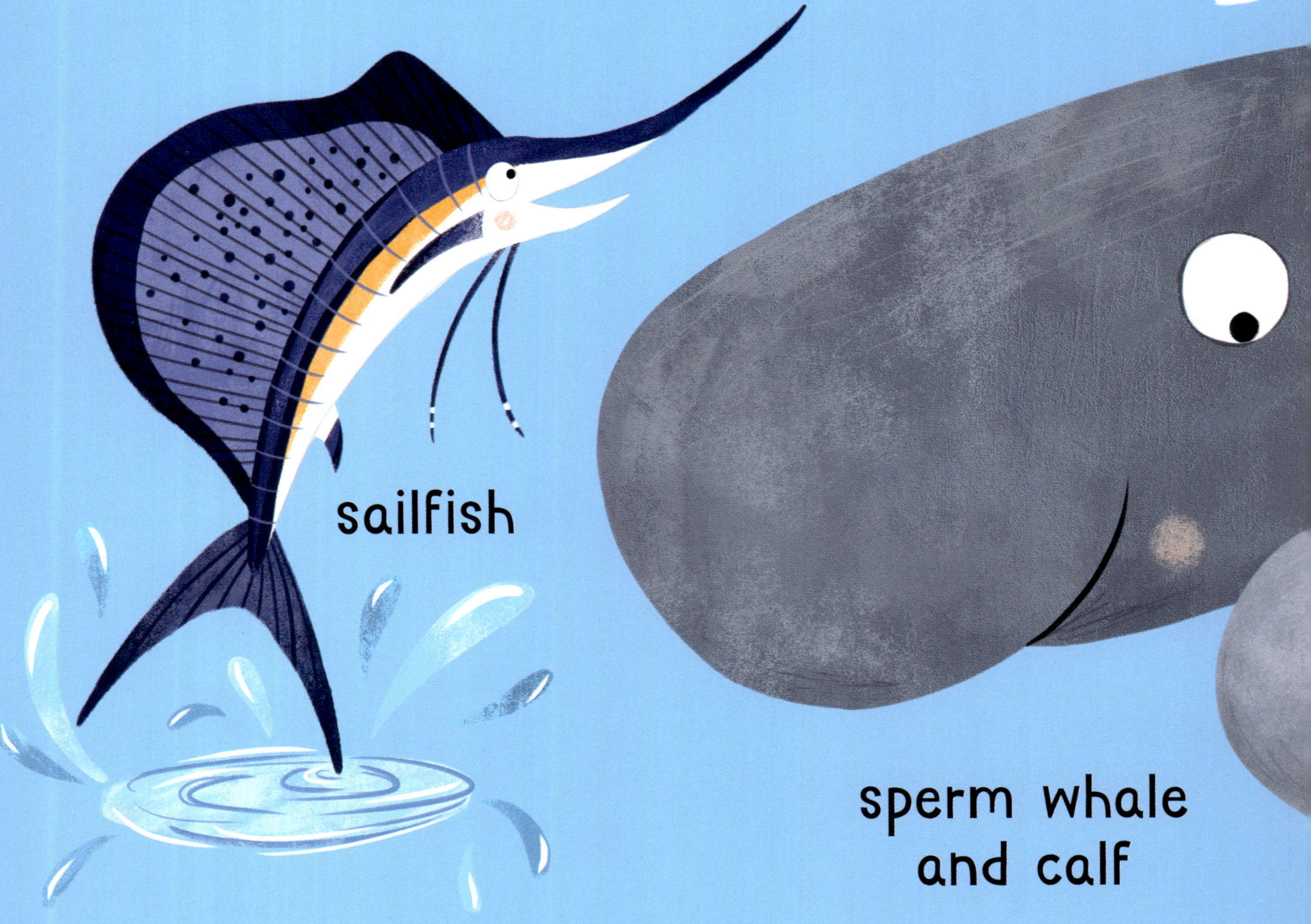

sailfish

sperm whale
and calf

swordfish
WHICH FISH IS LEAPING OUT OF THE WATER?
dolphin
13

As fish swim beneath the waves, seabirds fly above the surface.

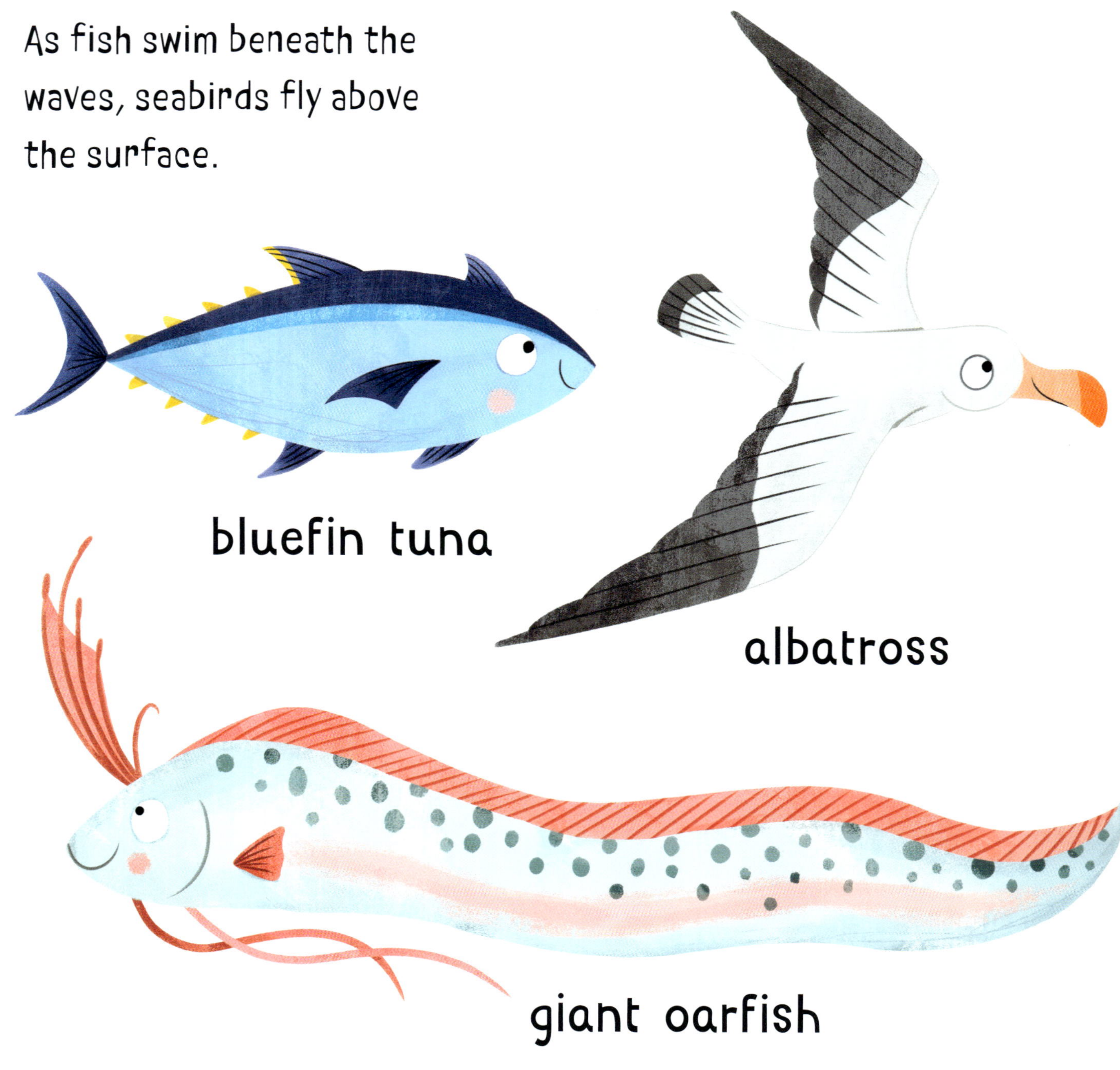

bluefin tuna

albatross

giant oarfish

14

CAN YOU COUNT THREE BIRDS?
haddock
beak
mackerel
flying fish
gannets

Icy seas and shores

The poles are at the north and south of the Earth. The seas here are very cold.

polar bear and cubs

orca
wings
Arctic tern
HOW MANY POLAR BEAR CUBS CAN YOU COUNT?
leopard seal
whiskers

Penguins, whales, and walruses
live in the icy polar lands.

penguins

chick

narwhal

18

WHICH CREATURE HAS ONE LONG TUSK?
king penguin
beluga whale
walrus
tusks

19

In deep water

Special submersibles explore the bottom of the deepest oceans.

dumbo
octopus

gulper
eel

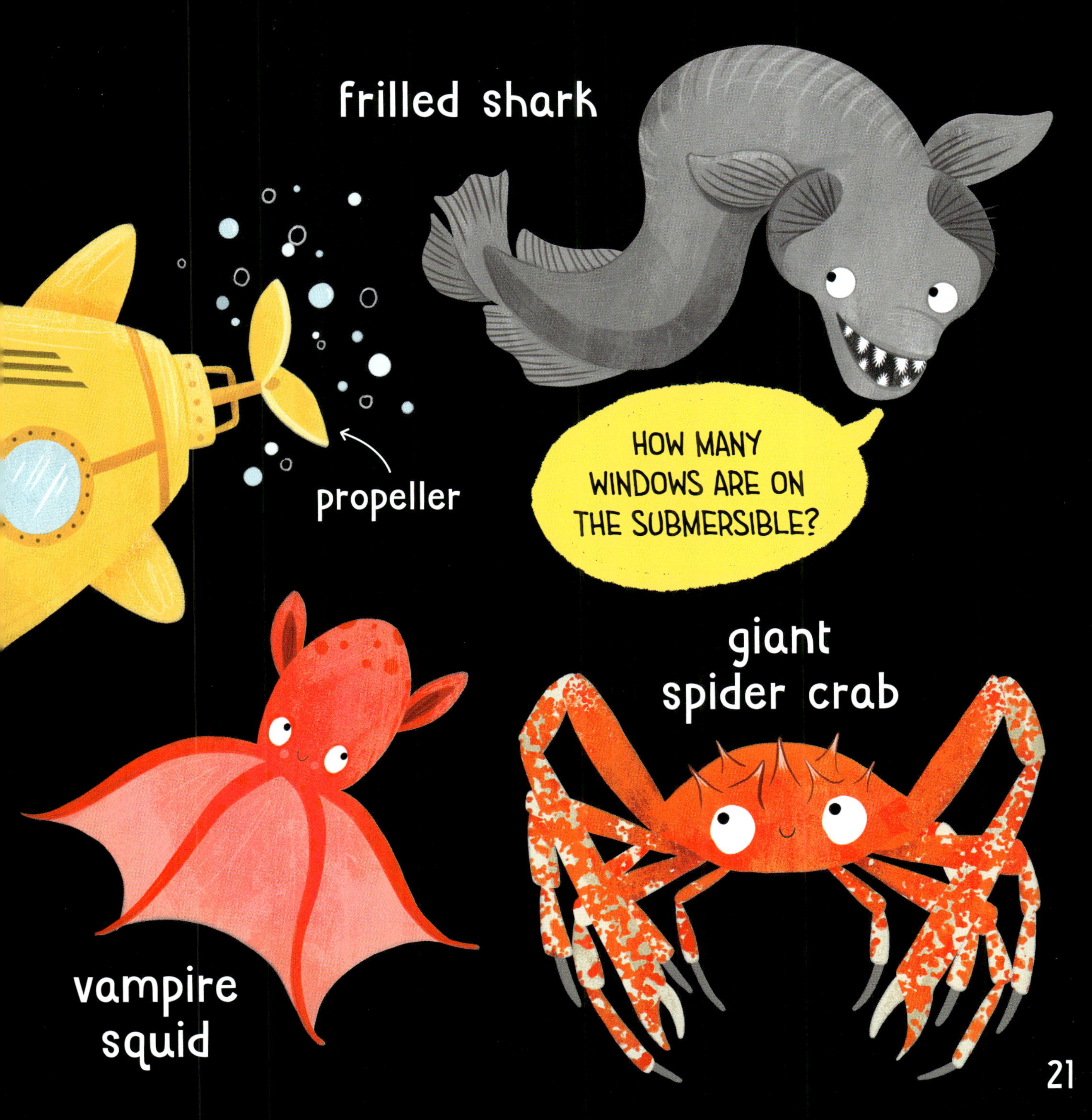

frilled shark
propeller
HOW MANY
WINDOWS ARE ON
THE SUBMERSIBLE?
giant
spider crab
vampire
squid
21

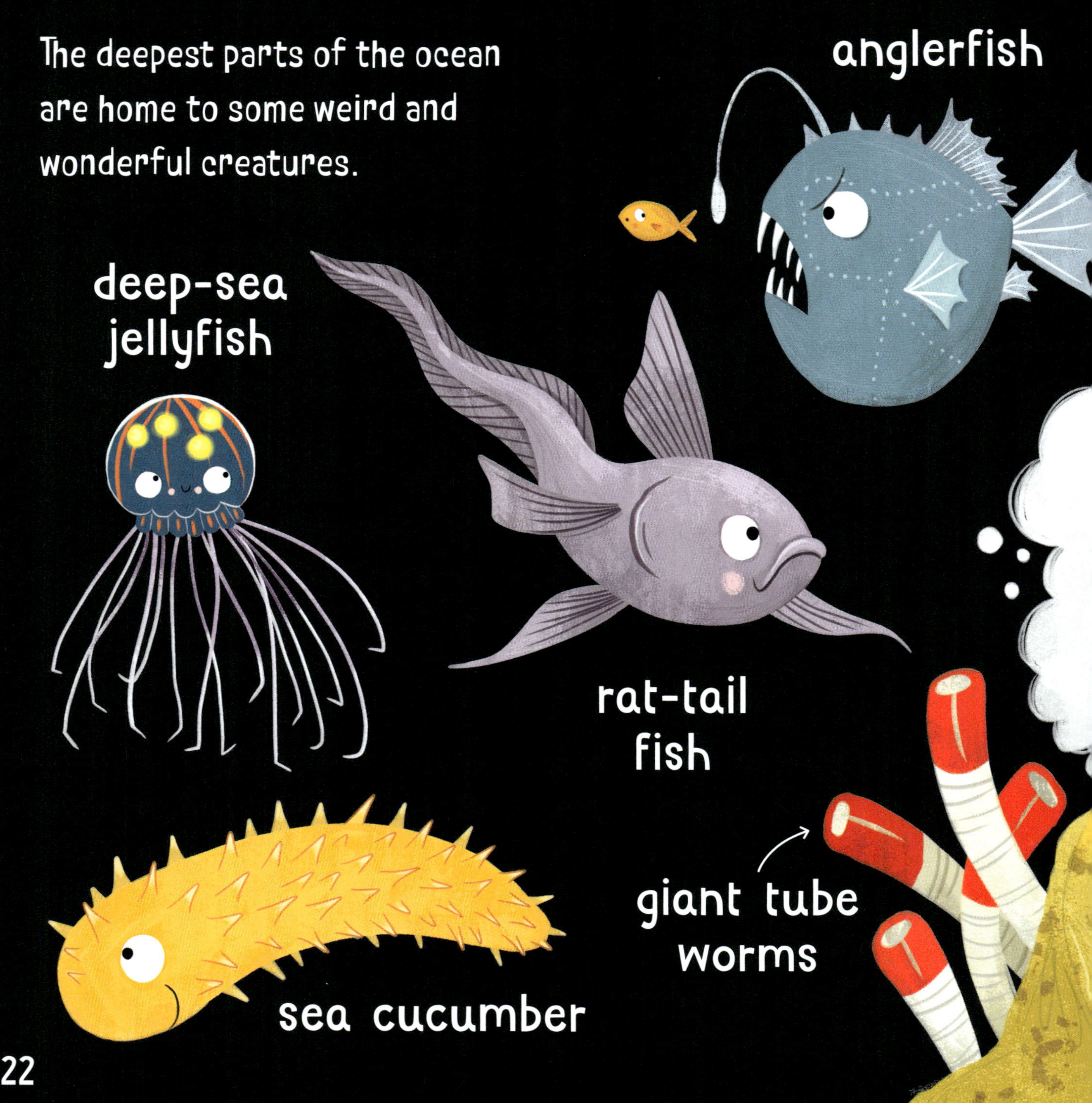

The deepest parts of the ocean are home to some weird and wonderful creatures.
anglerfish
deep-sea jellyfish
rat-tail fish
giant tube worms
sea cucumber

viperfish
giant squid
WHICH FISH IS CHASING ANOTHER FISH?
23

Ocean giants

Some ocean creatures are
absolutely enormous!

sunfish
manatee
giant manta ray

Seashore

There is a lot to spot along the seashore, where the land meets the sea.

loggerhead turtle
puffin
eggs
WHO IS LAYING
SOME EGGS?
seashells
shore
crab

Seashores can be rocky or sandy places. Many animals and plants live both in and out of the water.

CAN YOU SPOT THREE BEAKS?
seaweed
blue
jellyfish
HOW MANY SEA LIONS ARE ON THE ROCKS?

Rock pools

Found along rocky shores, these little pools of seawater are full of life.

sponge

rock pool

net

bucket

clams
sea anemone
goby
CAN YOU FIND TWO LITTLE STARFISH?
CAN YOU SPOT THE NET AND BUCKET?

Lots of different animals and plants
live in rock pools.

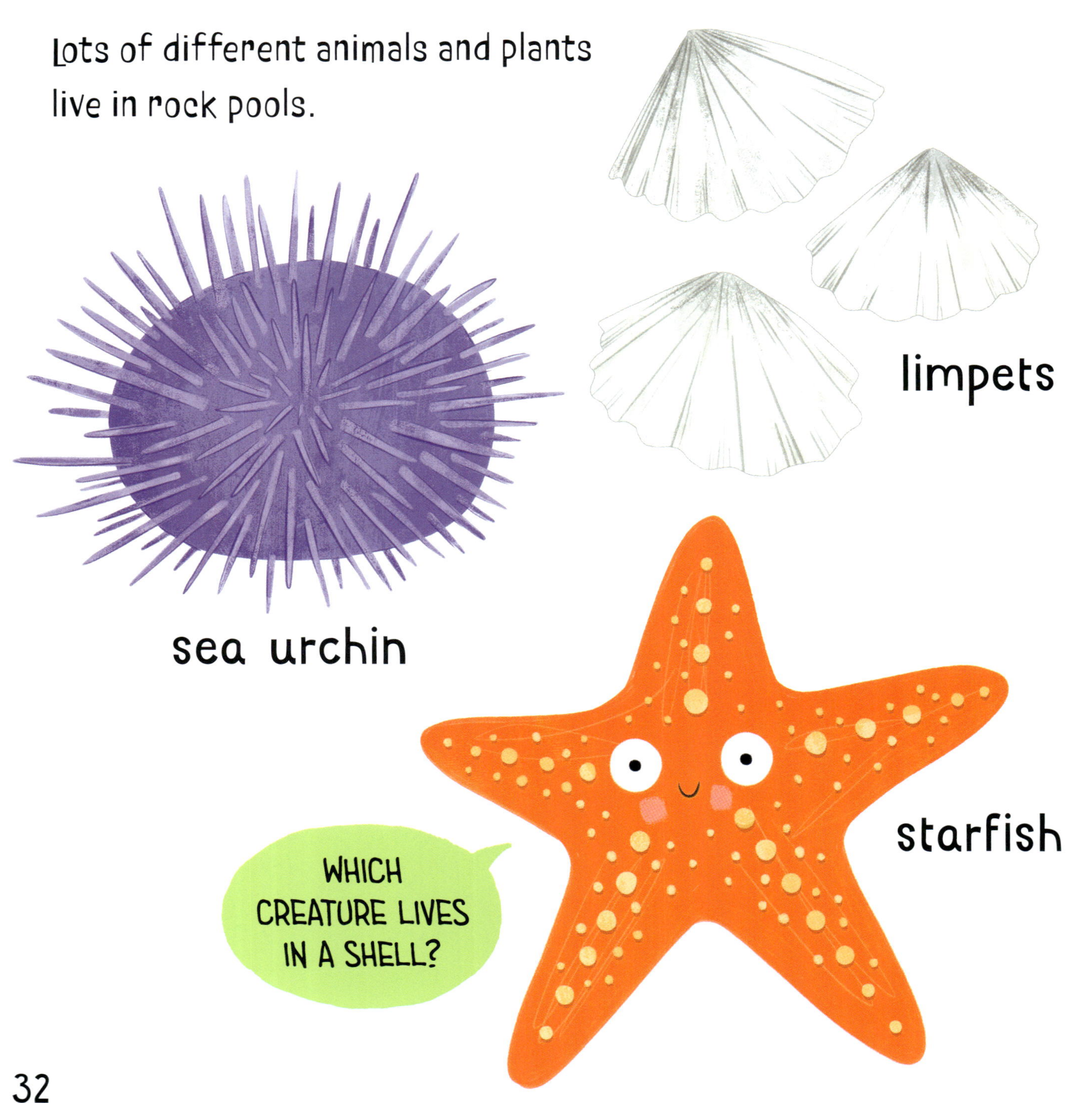

HOW MANY ARMS DOES THE STARFISH HAVE?
hermit crab
spiral wrack
seaweed
sugar kelp

Underwater forests

In some places, huge forests of kelp seaweed sway under the sea.

sea snail
kelp
kelp forest
HOW MANY ROCKFISH CAN YOU COUNT?

Mangrove trees grow in swamps by the sea and have big, tangly roots.

mudskipper

egret

lemon shark

alligator

HOW MANY CREATURES HAVE WINGS?

cormorant

mangrove swamp
tree roots

Shipwreck!

Deep at the bottom of the sea lie shipwrecks with buried treasure.

mast
oxygen tank
diver
porthole
wrasse
anchor

Lots of different sea creatures like living in and around shipwrecks.
leafy seadragon
WHICH FISH IS ORANGE?
sawfish
parrotfish
40

great white shark
sea slug
manta ray
lionfish

At the harbor

These are busy places where fishing boats are moored when not at sea.

cockles

brown crab

seagull
fishing boat
fishing rod
fisherman
lighthouse
jetty
seagull
43

You can find sea creatures like these in and around harbors.

cuttlefish

mussels

bream

mullet
HOW MANY MUSSELS CAN YOU COUNT?
plaice
seal and pup

Numbers

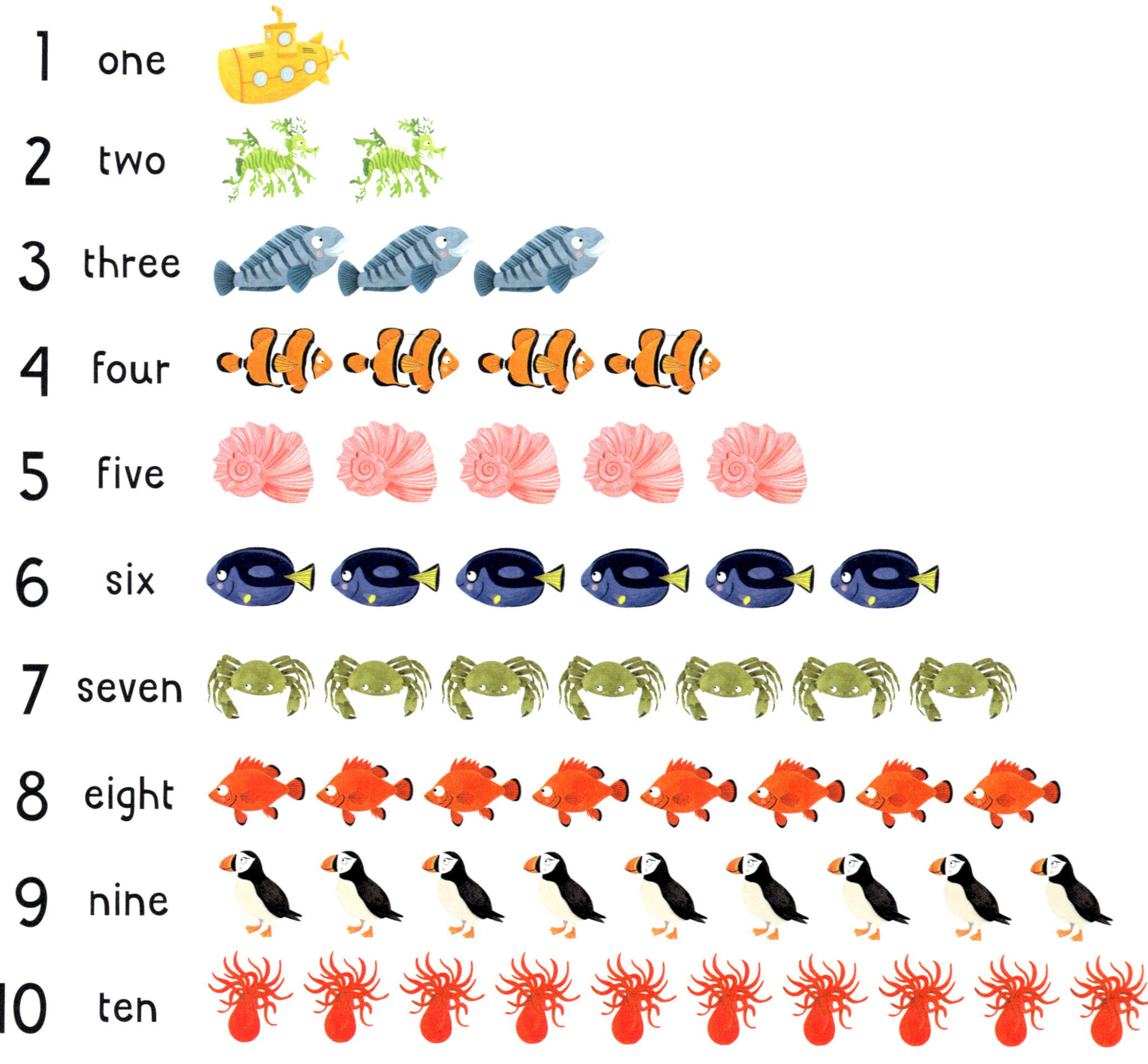

1	one
2	two
3	three
4	four
5	five
6	six
7	seven
8	eight
9	nine
10	ten

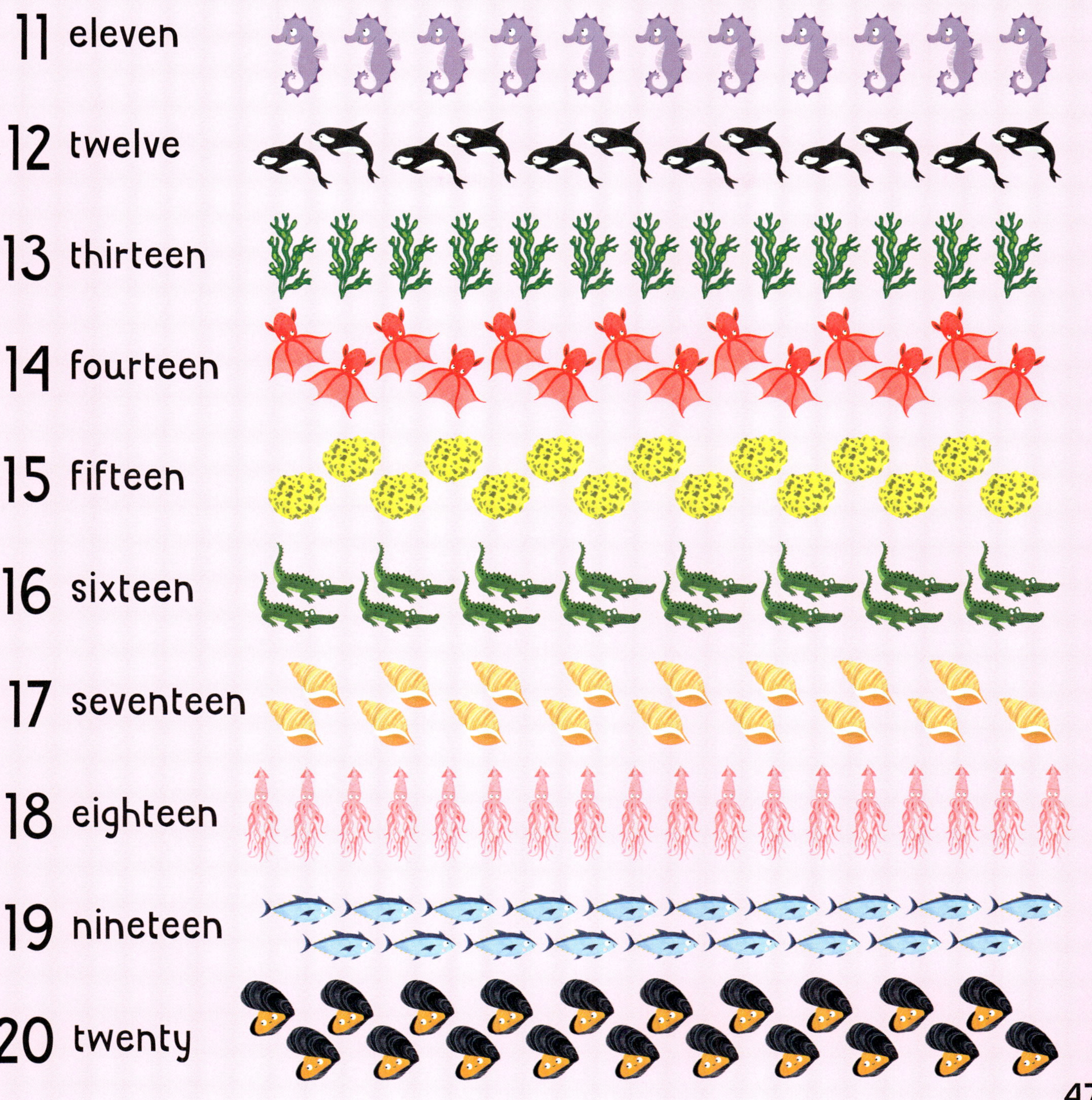

11	eleven
12	twelve
13	thirteen
14	fourteen
15	fifteen
16	sixteen
17	seventeen
18	eighteen
19	nineteen
20	twenty

Colors

white
beluga whale
silver
dolphin
orange
rock crab
blue
lobster
red
starfish
black
giant manta ray
yellow
sea slug
green
sea turtle
pink prawn
purple
sea urchin
brown
sea otter